THIS
PARTICULAR
ETERNITY

STEVE ORLEN

T0266022

AUSABLE PRESS
2001

Cover art: "Tuscany", oil on canvas (detail)
by Gail Marcus Orlen

Design and composition by Ausable Press.
The type is Van Dijck.
Cover design by Rebecca Soderholm.

Published by
AUSABLE PRESS
46 EAST HILL ROAD, KEENE NY 12942

www.ausablepress.com

The Acknowledgments appear on page 71 and
constitute a continuation of the copyrights page.

Library of Congress Control Number: 2001089397
ISBN 0-9672668-4-X (case; acid-free paper)
ISBN 978-096726-685-5 (pbk.; acid-free paper)

ALSO BY STEVE ORLEN

Sleeping on Doors. Penumbra Press, 1976
Separate Creatures. Ironwood Press, 1977
Permission to Speak. Wesleyan University Press, 1978
A Place at the Table. Holt, Rinehart, & Winston, 1981
The Bridge of Sighs. Miami University Press, 1992
Kisses. Miami University Press, 1997

THIS PARTICULAR ETERNITY

For Cozi and Gail
&
The Wise Uncle, Gibb Windahl

CONTENTS

Happy As I Am   1

Taboo   6

Onomastics & The Falling Snow   9

A War-Time Yard   12

Cruelty   16

Song: The Kiss   20

The Beach at Nice   23

Kristalnacht   24

Reverie: Foreign Movie in a Foreign Country   27

In the House of the Voice of Maria Callas   31

Gossip of the Inner Life   32

Ars Poetica   35

Monkey Mind   38

One-Man Band   39

Learning How to Look: Rilke & Rodin   41

The Painter   44

Butterflies That Save Us from Ourselves   46

The Great Wheel   48

Reverie: The Graveyard Shift   51

Reverie: *The Saturday Evening Post   55*

What I Found   59

My Blue Woman   61

Nature Rarely Confides in Me   64

Acknowledgements   71

HAPPY AS I AM

Trailer parks, projects, Circle K parking lots,
And trash-ridden vacant places,
And coldly-illuminated side streets with front porches
Peeling their rented paint. He's sullen. She's screaming. Two
       fat babies
Sit dazed on a couch. There's maybe a knife or a gun, and
       blood,
A few drops already scabbing on her face or pooled dry
On the sidewalk, mapping a wound, and it's always after-
       wards,
Ten minutes later, a half hour.
                        Every night I watch the
    show *Cops*
After dinner. I'm by myself because it upsets my wife, the
       voyeurism
Of it, the high-pitched, tension emergency sounds,
And my son, a good boy who by now has fallen far from the
       tree,
Hates the unpredictability, the chaos, and blood, *especially the
       blood*,
He says, but he loves the verbal violence of rap music, so who
       knows
How far he's fallen,
                  and I love the opening rasta song, *Bad
  Boys*,
Because that's what I thought I always was, what my father
       called me
As a boy, the neighbors, too, the relatives, the principal of
       the junior high

1

Who told my father on the phone, *You don't have to worry about*
Your son going to college, he's going to jail, and hung up.

Why do you watch that stuff? my wife asks from the kitchen.
Because I feel I sort of *know* these people, from childhood—
The perps, the cops, the victims—
Especially when they show the smaller cities,
Like the one I grew up in, Holyoke, Massachusetts, which is not
This TV city in fact, so the show is both real and not real
And I can believe whatever I want. I'm waiting to see
Someone I used to know, one of the screw-offs, the junior high
Falling-down-drunks, the burglars, window-smashers, car stealers,
Famous street fighters, the greater and the lesser clowns, those in groups
And those mysterious maniacs who worked alone. Those people gathered
On the television porch, still arguing, the very sullen, bare-chested man
In close-up with *SUGAR* tattooed over one nipple and *CREAM*
Over the other, and the very frightened, dispossessed-looking
Plump woman biting her nails, and through the screen door
Three children asleep on a couch, crumpled like pieces of dropped paper
Nobody notices, and the cops—I think if I look closer
I'll recognize one of them.
I know that woman smothered in light on the front porch
Because I went out with her once.

Actually, I sat next to her *doppelganger*
In the Victory Theatre on one of those Friday nights
When all the kids went to the movies in summer.
Her name was always *Bunny*
Or *Beverly*, one sitting on my right and one on my left,
Shadows only, in profile, and after the opening credits

I put my arm around Bunny's shoulder and we started kiss-
     ing,
And then I felt her up. I didn't know her. I couldn't even
Quite see her face, but I liked the slight glow of her, and the
     girl-smell
Of her rose petal soap, and the way her girlfriend nibbled
At her cuticles and watched us instead of the movie,
Until I turned to her and we went at it, too, back and forth
     like that.

And now she—Beverly, Bunny, I can't tell—is on TV,
Famous for several minutes in a humiliating scene, almost
     live
And pretty much unedited, with a long slash on her right
     cheek
And a smudged bump on her pale forehead, and she seems—
Not happy, of course—but *in* it, in her life,
While one cop is taking notes on a pad and another
Is frisking the squirming man, asking
Do you have any needles in your pockets, sir?

Someone you can't see is filming the whole slow chaos
With an unsteady hand, panning to
The small crowd gathered like a chorus in their night-
     clothes,

And the red lights twirling, surveilling. The cops are being
    nice to everyone.
They're used to this. They know they're on TV. They've
    taken courses
In courtesy. With a bit of bad luck or a wrong turn taken
It could have been them being frisked and cuffed on some
    Hillside Avenue.

Sometimes, proudly, I tell my son stories
About our burglaries at "midnight lumber," then one siren
    coming in,
Then the voices exploding at us like those inchers on the
    Fourth of July,
The running, scrambling over back fences, hiding, the
    whispered laughing,
While the cops looked for us desultorily, though if caught
We would get a smack or two.
                                    The woman is mumbling
    something
We can't hear in our living rooms. I *know*
She is either Beverly or Bunny, though whatever was glowing
    about her,
Whatever innocence comprised her being,
Has dimmed to a cold illumination
On a front porch. Somebody in me is hearing her say,
Hey, Turk–they used to call me Turk–*Why don't you*
Come out and join us, or *Why are you out there*
And I'm in here on your television set? Or *Are you happy in your*
    life?
Actually, she's laughing, mildly, inaudibly, at her situation of
    this night.

It's just life. *Everybody's life is just life, right?* she seems to be
        saying.
And *Some nights you're in the chorus and some nights*
You're in the middle of the mess, right?
                                        My wife
Has put the cookies out to cool. To some rap
My son is break-dancing for me, interrupting my favorite
        show,
Irritating me on purpose. *How do you like that move?* he asks.
It's a good one, pal, I tell him, very happy with how he's
        turning out,
But wondering, stupidly, why he's not like me, out in the
        street
Getting into trouble, and wondering why I'm watching
        strangers on TV,
Peeping through a keyhole into the alternate universe.

Happy as I am, happy as anyone is, I still have this urge
To be with Beverly tonight, with Bunny, too.
Not on that front porch, but in the chorus
Where not a word is spoken.
No thinking much. Only the body's chemical fuming.
Only a movie theater where half the kids are necking
Furiously and the other half watching, and Bunny and
        Beverly and I
Are touching each other in a twisted, anonymous passion
Within the smells of Beverly's soap, the cigarette smoke in
        Bunny's
Endlessly long brown hair, their urgent sweat, their lips,
        their lipstick,
The sweet-sweet candy everyone around us is sucking on.

⦿ TABOO

In this photograph of my mother,
Posed and taken by my father
Several years before I was born, when they were

Or were not yet married,
Depending upon who is telling the story,
My mother is standing, is still standing

Because of the way photographs make chumps of us,
And you have only to reach out and take her hand
And tell her *it's time to get moving,*

Get dressed, honey, we're going home—
My mother stands with her long back, flank and legs
To the camera and her face both haughty and coy in profile

In front of a mass of mountain rock
Under an opaque, embellishing waterfall
Whose drops scatter over her shoulders.

She is wearing nothing but a white bathing cap,
Which I imagine was either a bow to nicety
Or a brilliant, perverse touch of my father's.

The photograph, in black and white, circa 1931,
Has been enlarged, and so is a bit grainy,
And it seems as though her smooth back, which conspires

With the water to make her appear even more beautiful
And more vulnerable to the eye, is disintegrating,
Although she is quite young, maybe seventeen.

I will know from later photographs that her hair
Tucked under the cap is full and auburn and long
With waves here and there in an unruly falling,

And I would never see her actual body
But I know her breasts are as large and over-ripe
As *melons in a field*

Because my proud father told me this as a child,
And because lately, in her old age, she complains
That her breasts pull her shoulders down

In a traitorous falling, and make them ache.
They're my burden, she said last night in the kitchen,
Holding them up in both hands, smiling,

As though what was once pride is still pride,
But the exempting pride
Of having outlived the body, the naked and shapely,

As yet unrepentant, distracting body
Shimmering and disintegrating
In this old photograph I dug up

From the bottom of the pile
In the basement of my parents' house.
My father, at eighty-seven, is blind

And emaciated and slowly metastasizing,
Upstairs in his narrow bed, dying.
And my mother, at eighty-three,

Is for this particular eternity
The beautiful, water-splashed
Woman in this photograph. It both embarrasses me

And draws me in. The thick black
Leather-bound cover of the album is embossed
With a golden bird, a blazing phoenix

Hesitating in its upwards flight,
Drawn for a moment to its ashes down below
Before it moves on, as it surely must.

☉ ONOMASTICS & THE FALLING SNOW

Most everything has a name except the falling snow,
        By which I mean each flake, each one different,
As one spirit is different from another, and close up,
        Under a microscope, crystalline, like a thing made
By a master watchmaker with a motor the size
        Of a fingernail and an awl as fine as a hair.

Sillier men than I have tried to name the flakes of snow
        While standing hatless at a bus stop, watching the
                snow
Fall on apple trees and oaks, making them all the same.
        Did you know that among the ancient Hebrew tribes
Children were given two names at birth,
        One sacred, one profane? The child wasn't told

The sacred one. So he walked around with two names,
        One by which to be called in from the sheepfold
And the other intricate, mysterious, useless.
        And in Norway, circa early twentieth century,
There were so few hereditary names to pass down
        Everyone must have thought everyone else a cousin.

Maybe that's why they're so polite, so orderly, and why,
        If it's snowing in Oslo, there will always be
A helpful soul standing beside you to offer space
        The size of an umbrella while waiting for the bus.
In America a name means nothing—a marker to be called in,
        A convenience: Mr. Weaver may not be at his loom,

Nor Mr. Lavender making soap. Nor does anyone remember
        Herr Gross, the fat man who stood in line waiting for
The greedy minions of the fanatic Empress Maria Theresa
        To take his money and bestow upon him a name
To be passed down to fat and skinny children alike.
        And if a man were even poorer, and as a mean joke,

He might be called the German equivalent of *Grease*,
        Or *Monkey Weed* or *Do Not Borrow From* or *Gallows Rope*.
In Russia, in 1802, to raise an army, Czar Alexander
        Sent out a ukase ordering each Jew to take a last
            name—
It must have been like writing a poem, mind-sprung
        And wholly inspired on first draft, then inscribing it

On the forehead of a neighbor, each one befitting:
        Eiseman, for *He Who Laughs*, or Mazal, *Lucky Man*,
Or Trubnic for *Chimney Sweep*, or Soroka *The Magpie*,
        Meaning *The Gossip*. And babies in those days
Were sometimes given ugly names to turn aside
        The assiduous, bureaucratic Angel of Death;

Or, in illness, a child was renamed to befuddle
        The same angel coming down with his empty sack
To collect for God's heavens. But naming the snow,
        Each flake, each deliquescing cryptic coat of arms,
That would be a game for only the most inventive,
        Hopeless man. For after all, the snowflakes

Are the soon-to-be-dead, those who float awhile
    Then fall and, merging, pile up like corpses
On some northern battlefield, and there melt, flow
    Down as water to the river that has one name only.
It so happens it's snowing where I'm standing now
    At a bus stop in Oslo, between one moment and the
    next,

Feeling nostalgic, homesick, trying to remember the names
    Of everyone I've ever known. Hopeless, of course.
So it worries me that my son, who is more like me
    Than I care to think about, could recite the names
Of each child in his kindergarten class after only one week
    Of sitting with his hands folded on his desk.

He wasn't praying, he told me. He was waiting
    For the names to sink in so one morning he could say,
Suddenly, to each one, *Hi*, because it's good
    To be remembered. By the time we are old
We can baptize each flake before the bus arrives.
    There are so many people to know by name,

So many... They grew away from me.
    They became snow, fuzzy at this distance,
Just beyond my reach, waiting to be called upon again.

@A WAR-TIME YARD

I'm trying to perfect the art of looking backward
Without nostalgia. The art of recalling
What's important, and to whom, what rises on its own.
A little kid's face, say, with a certain
Focused, outward-leaning look, rising from sleep
In summer; or even a bird, at first appearance meaningless,
      yanking
A nightcrawler out of the early morning earth.

I'm thinking about a simple and for a while timeless
Backyard that could have been yours, or anyone's,
Though it was mine, and therefore a sentimental
Quarter acre of dirt. No one watered it,
Except for rain, and the little kids tromped on it
While playing the games they played before
The games got organized, and before the World War was over.

Every summer a small, single clump
Of weedy-looking rhubarb grew, and every summer
The kids were surprised with a steaming pie
The lonely old lady on the third floor baked for them.
In German, her name meant *farmer*.
And in America at that time, her name meant
Dirt.
      There are certain details in a minor mode
That rise, like morning fog as it rises and exposes:
A lilac glade, loud with yellow jackets
And darning needles that threatened any kid who told a lie,
Whose chore it was to wake the kids on summer mornings.
And when the cheap perfume of lilac globes emerged

It seemed they'd always been there, like Christmas orna-
      ments
Packed in flock and waiting in the parlor closet,
Because the kids were too young
Still to notice change as a way of being, and anyway
Nothing much changed in that neighborhood in those times,
Except for the course of the war itself,
And that only in whispers and obituaries.

The lady upstairs might have had a relative involved,
Or might not. But the jagged profile
Of her German accent marked her as *enemy*,
Even three floors up hanging her laundry
On the back porch line, calling down *Gut morning!*

From the first branch of the elm kids could see
Over the narrow span of a six foot fence,
And so they began to climb it too, and once
On the other side, they climbed back. Keeping that world,
I suppose, boundaried and repeatedly recoverable.
This was a game before the games got organized, before
There were rules to remember and to follow,
Before there was even history
Because the fathers were still mythical,

And all of this represents
Both a stilled recollection and a single season, summer,
Or maybe a couple of summers, with the family of skunks
The kids could see from the bedroom window at night
With their broad white insolent stripes lighting up the yard
And the kids would sniff that ripe, ineradicable, comic stink.
Where the skunks went in daytime, no kid knew
And no kid was curious or old enough

13

To care yet.
                    This was what the neighbors referred to
As a *war-time yard*. Not a single blade of grass,
Only the hardy dandelions people were re-learning
How to make a bitter salad of; no barbecue yet,
No picnic table, only the widow's *Victory Garden*
Led to on a path between the weeds;
While underground the black dirt harbored
Nightcrawlers, though no kid fished yet
Because most of the fathers were off to war, and anyway
The kids were too squeamish to thread those slimy,
Baited, peristaltic bodies onto a barbed hook,
And because the lady upstairs yelled down
In gutturals to leave them alone.
                                    If you stand staring
For a while in the stupid sated haze of after-supper
You can see these things as they arise, can hear them
Like names called out, like themes of a fugue that only
        organize
If you want them to. You can keep them
Or you can return them, back where they belong.

I don't believe a grown-up ever even noticed this yard
As anything more than an artless mess,
Because everyone was busy at the factories.
That winter, I'll bet there was never even a footprint
In the snow, while underneath the ground froze,
The rhubarb's roots did whatever rhubarb's roots
Do in winter, gathering the sour with the sweet,
Until the snow melted, and the dense dirt began to thaw so
        loud
You could hear the rocks crack, and buds and leaves came
        out,

14

Looking like trinkets on a girl's bracelet, and the sow bugs
Bumped their blind way under stones, and the days
Grew so gradually longer no one noticed, and then the war,
The long war was over. There was a parade downtown,
And people shouted. Everyone wore a button.
New faces were seen on the streets, faces hardened
And puzzled by what had become of their children
Who didn't seem to know them, who didn't obey as promptly
As the fathers had in war;
                              and the fathers,
Who had learned the arts of war without
Yet gaining the fortunes of war, began to organize.
Leagues were formed, chores doled out, loud words
Could be heard behind closed doors, haircuts got so short
They resembled lawns, and one Saturday morning
The man of the house I'm trying to remember
Without nostalgia, although nostalgia has such a pretty face,
Even without the make-up the mothers began to wear again,
The returned father rummaged in the back of the garage
And found a burlap bag of grass seed, a rusty sickle
And a hoe, a lawn mower and a can of *Three-In-One Oil*,
And when the rhubarb lady died, her German name, *Bauer*,
       meaning *farmer*,
Was pried, after a decent interval, off the front door,
And the grass grew high, and the grass got mown.

CRUELTY

Because we were all sweaty,
And irritable, and in a sort of jerky hurry
Like junkies always are, my friend, and the dope dealer
And his girlfriend the dying woman, and me
Who always came along, I'm sure it was summer,

And also because
I remember the smell of the nose-opening ether
They used to cut heroin with
Mixing with the bitter, smelly, Grape-Ade effusions
Off the purple flowers of a jacaranda tree
Whose top brushed the window
Of the dealer's third-floor apartment,
And the tingle of mold that rises from a carpet
When spring is over.
               The dying woman
Was a short black stub dressed like a clerk
Or a secretary on her lunch break,
Someone who works every day without complaint, and
      because
I didn't know her very well I could say that maybe
She also lived in a run-down dump like this,
With a lumpy sofa she slept on and a TV set
And a table with one wooden chair for eating, but I imagine
She kept her place clean, dusted and swept
Because that's how she looked
With her flowered blouse tucked in
And her straight skirt pulled below her knees,
Even as she was nodding into an overdose,

Like someone falling into an afternoon nap,
Until the nodding stopped
And her head spasmed and jerked back, and her eyes,
Stuck open for a moment, showed only the whites.

When the dealer began slapping her hard across the face
I knew there was no cruelty in it, only panic,
And beneath the panic the sure knowledge of his trade.
When he stripped off her blouse and pinched her purple
        nipples
Hard enough to almost tear them off too,
There was no cruelty in that either.

I can only picture her now
As a rag doll being tortured by a frightened child,
The way the dying woman's body
Moved only when the dealer moved it,
Then, failing to revive her, he lugged her dead weight
Into the shower and ran ice cold water
Over her half-naked body
Which was so black I thought it too was purple,
Glistening under the shower's spray.

The dealer positioned himself like a boxer,
He set his feet just so
And jabbed methodically
At her wet and slippery body, and while we watched
She kept falling and the dealer kept lifting her up
To lean her against the wall, unbearably.
This is when it happened, the one moment
I keep thinking about, like a window
Within a window on a terrible event:

My friend picked up
The dying woman's black plastic imitation patent leather
        purse
From the floor, and rifled it,
And held up the small wad of bills
Like a birthday present to himself
Or a prize won at the amusement park, and grinned at me,
Then we moved on to the next connection's apartment
And bought some dope and I watched him shoot it up.

We always, afterwards, walked around a lot. We always
        stopped
To play with the little kids on the street.
We'd talk and flirt with that buzzing knot of girls
Who hung around in front of the grocery store.
Maybe we'd bait a barking dog, or talk with a vagrant
To hear where he had been. The woman died. I don't know
What happened to the dealer. My friend is dead now too,
Ten years later shot in the chest in an alley
By a teenage boy he was blackmailing for being queer,
And if anyone got what he deserved
My friend did, if ever you can say such a thing.

And what about me, you might ask. I didn't run
To the telephone, if there even was one, and dial 911,
Which they didn't have back then, and yell, *Hey
There's a woman here dying of an overdose!*

I didn't do any more than shake my head
And purse my lips like a schoolteacher
At a naughty boy.
                Let's go get in trouble,
He used to say, afterwards, after the dope

And the walking, and the little bouts of talk,
And we'd move on. Moving on. That was it. That was
The cruel thing I did in those days.

◉ SONG: THE KISS

We were walking through
      A department store in Paris,
Escaping the rain,
      The sort of French rain
That changes in intensity
      If you look at it,
Then changes back if you don't.
      You went to lingerie,
And I to electronics,
      And then we met again. It was there
That you noticed them, in furnishings,
      Relaxing on a couch, his arm
Draped around her shoulder.
      She pecked him on the cheek.
He didn't seem to notice.
      Practicing for marriage,
You said, a bit too wryly
      I thought, then stared at them
With you. He was pompadoured,
      Italian, rough and beautiful,
With muscles so prominent
      They seemed to be tattooed,
And you must have felt a twinge
      Moving up your throat
To your face, for it settled
      Into a smile, half adoration,
Half resignation. And she, Italianate,
      Shapely as that ivory statue

Pygmalian called "my virgin beauty,"
　　　　With hair so long and black
I could almost see myself
　　　　Reflected in it, and behind me
You watching me watching
　　　　Her small breasts move
Beneath her black t-shirt.
　　　　Then on we went, you to where
The silk scarves were,
　　　　All the rage that year,
And I to toys to see
　　　　What passed for toys those days,
And then we met again,
　　　　By the escalator, and out
The revolving doors we went,
　　　　Hand in hand, for this was Paris,
Where even the middle-aged
　　　　Will behave like young lovers
In the rain, waiting for bad weather
　　　　To bring them to their youth again.
And there they were, standing
　　　　In the rain that hadn't changed
For an hour. They were kissing,
　　　　Their tongues wrestling
In that eternal battle
　　　　No one wins or loses.
His hand was on her breast,
　　　　Cupping it; her hand on top of his,
As if to keep it there forever
　　　　Were a commitment they'd just now taken on.
And you said, laughing,
　　　　If you let me kiss him
I'll let you kiss her!

Then we set out again,
Hand in hand, thirty years married,
    Across the busy Seine,
And then I was the one laughing,
    And you, I thought for a moment
You were crying,
    But it was only the rain in Paris,
Relentless and unchanging.

◉ THE BEACH AT NICE

Up on the boardwalk, fully-dressed, the poor are staring, who
      can't afford the beach,
And think this is the orchard of breasts their mothers'
      bodies offered,
The melons and plums, the pears and others.
They smoke and chat and run their glances down
The long and rocky line of shore and back.
They laugh, compare, these connoisseurs, their conversation
      serious.
With hands cupped open, they approximate. Lacking the
      means, they yearn.
Lacking a camera, they take a snapshot with the eye
Then on thin bikes rush home, eating their hearts out with
      pleasure.

⦿ KRISTALNACHT

It was Rome. I was out walking with my mother-in-law.
She was telling me that in her youth, in Frankfurt,
Before the war and during the Nazis, she loved sweets.
Loved them so much she worried she would die on
      Kristalnacht
Because of a single lump of hard candy. She imagined
Dying must be something like that,
A melting inward, until you were dead, but blissfully so.

"I was only twelve years old that night,
And I was by myself, walking around the city. My dress
Was blue and too big for my body.
I was hoping to grow up to be a teenager..."
As she talked we kept walking, a vague and pleasant night,
Late autumn, and she was just getting started,
Already getting lost
In the detail of a blue, flower-printed dress,
Which to her meant more than the story,
Kristalnacht, night of the breaking glass,

And I knew we were already getting lost in the city,
Going uphill, then walking across a darkened plaza
At the edge of and overlooking the city; the lights
Below ran in rivers, then islands, then rivers again,
Holding it all together; and the dim figure
Of a man in overalls was sweeping leaves
With a broad broom in brisk motions
Away from a small dry fountain toward the edge of the plaza.

Across the city, crazed islands
Of light pulsed, flared up and dimmed, like fires,
So I prodded her to keep telling me about *Kristalnacht*.

"We'd been warned, so my mother handed me
Some *Reichmarks*, and her wedding band, and she walked
In one direction and I in the opposite, and she said
We would meet back here at dawn, if we were still alive,
But she didn't tell me where we would meet if we weren't—
Alive, that is—and that puzzle occupied me as I walked,
First through familiar, then unfamiliar streets, whose names
I memorized and still remember—*Freir von Stein Strasse,
Staufen Strasse, Unter Lindau, Reuterwag.*

"And so all night I watched from different distances
The synagogues blaze up toward God, or so I imagined,
And listened to the child's exciting crash of breaking glass,
And wondered exactly who was doing it, throwing stones,
Which names rested on their tongues, which names
They answered to, if I knew their daughters, and what might
They be doing now, tonight, and what I might ask them,
Or if I would snub them entirely.

"All night I sucked on a lump of hard cherry candy I'd found
In the pocket of that dress. I would suck a while,
Then take it out and hold it
In the palm of my hand as I walked, not knowing where
I was headed, hoping for a circle,
Then suck a while longer. On and off all night I sucked
And didn't suck, to make it last until dawn,
And then I would be alive, not dead. I was extra careful, very

Disciplined, very German, even, stoical, because I thought
I was saving my mother, too. I kept asking myself,
Would they actually kill a little girl, all by herself,
In the middle of the night, sucking on a cherry candy..."

And there we were with that question, at the top of a city.
We were on vacation. My wife, her daughter,
Was back at the hotel, sleeping, and we
Were probably lost. We watched a small mutt
Slink across the stones, dragging its belly,
And since to my mother-in-law all dogs alone are lost dogs,
Just as all children alone are lost children, I had
To grip her arm to keep her from pursuing, and she laughed—
At me, I guessed, and at herself, and at a world
That can lose such treasures as dogs and children.

But what about the candy? I asked. Did it last you all night?
"No," she said, "I cheated!"
And laughed again. Then tore loose
From my grip and ran after that dog.
It was eleven at night, on the dot. For her sake
I will say that bells were ringing all over the city.

REVERIE: FOREIGN MOVIE IN
A FOREIGN COUNTRY
for Reg Gibbons

There is something innocent and indecent about a foreigner
Watching a movie in a small village in a foreign country.
Outdoors in a light rain at evening in summer,
Wearing a hat different from the local hats.
A tourist who got off the train because the place
Looked both quaint and hopelessly backward.

I noticed from my window
In my room in the only hotel in town, the local people,
Whole families, some with hats, some under huge
Umbrellas, walking slowly toward the square,
And the chairs being set out in crooked rows
By an old man and a little girl, and the people sitting,
As if they knew by long tradition which seat
Belonged to whom,

                    and I went down to join them,
Thinking at first a religious event commemorating,
Say, the patron saint of the village, some medieval nun
Who lived and died so this village could finally have
Both a name and an atmosphere of continual sacrifice,
Or a political speech by some functionary from Rome
Offering a new spray for the apple orchards,
Or maybe a mime, I hoped for a mime, for the way a mime
Will mirror the hopes, the foibles and shames
Of a people through the ease of communal embarrassment.
I sat among them. Around me it was very quiet at first,
Hushed, as the light of the projector in its portable booth
Came on in a straight line filled with the day's dust

Aimed at ten sewn-together spotty white bed sheets
Hanging down from the earthquake-cracked side
Of the church.
                                The movie was, by the mix
Of soft with dissonant music
Crackling out of two loudspeakers, a love story,
And tragic, and not in the local Italian but in a language
I didn't recognize, nor did the audience, it seemed.
No subtitles, either,
Although this didn't seem to bother anyone.
                                                    There was

A villain, a boss, immediately recognizable by his arched
Eyebrows and the short whip he carried from scene
To scene in his left hand; and the lovers,
Lovely to look at and young, as lovers
Always are in old movies, their faces bathed in light
In certain scenes, back-lit into darkness in others;

And there were large families seeming always to stand
Behind the lovers, like a chorus, dressed in the black
Clothes common to peasants anywhere and at any time
In Europe, in and out of mourning, or as if mourning
Were a perpetual condition of the poor.
                                        Something
Was sometimes going right and always going wrong
In the movie: a lost sheep ringing its bell
Caught in a sloped ravine, and money changing hands,
The palms up in close-ups, and shots of sudden lightning
In a brooding black and white sky, representing
The work of the gods, and then the pigeons
Frightened up into the air by a rifle shot,

And immediately afterwards, a coffin
Followed by a small cortege, also the chorus—

and I thought
For a flickering moment
That it's not right for the gods to behave worse
Than a man—

and so on, all the certain visual rhythms be-
longing
To certain kinds of moments, the sacramental,
The polluted, the ordinary.

But what was odd
And hopelessly foreign to me was not the chorus
In the movie but the chorus watching the movie.
How they seemed to know, without the benefit
Of local language, exactly what was going on, and why:
When to boo, snicker, hiss, when to light
A cigarette, when to laugh or cry.

They did all this
In unison, like a chorus, together, as a village,
Without a word or gesture to each other,
Living what I felt to be an idyllic
And tragic, tranced, country-rhythmed life,
Knowing exactly which sacrament was being re-enacted,
Which pollution dissipated by this sacrifice,
And to which god;

and, incorporated
Into the local drama, and because I felt lonely
And in need of something ordinary,
I, too, seemed to know it, after a while
And almost ahead of time, know which
Appropriate gesture to make,
So I felt almost at home, living a common story

While the pigeons cooed from their roosts
And the women wept with private happiness
And the men re-adjusted their hats
And shook with public laughter.

IN THE HOUSE OF THE VOICE
OF MARIA CALLAS

In the house of the voice of Maria Callas
We hear a baby's cries, and the after-supper
Rattle of silverware, and three clocks ticking
To different tunes, and ripe plums
Sleeping in their chipped bowl, and traffic sounds
Dissecting the avenues outside. And we hear, like water
Pouring over *time* itself, the pure distillate arias
Of the numerous pampered queens who have reigned,
And the working girls who have suffered
The envious knives, and the breathless brides
With their horned helmets who have fallen in love
And gone crazy or fallen in love and died
On the grand stage at their appointed moments,
And who will sing of them now? Maria Callas is dead,
Although the full lips and slanting eyes
And flaring nostrils of her voice resurrect
Dramas we are able to imagine in this parlor
On evenings like this one, adding some color,
Adding some order. Of whom it was said:
She could imagine almost anything and give voice to it.

GOSSIP OF THE INNER LIFE
for David Rivard

My good friend who these days despises the newspapers
Complains they aren't news but gossip, a talking down,
In brief sidebars, in the mathematics of the intellect,
From the highest to the lowest common denominator,
The front pages with their treaties signed and breached
In an afternoon, the borders fixing and unfixing themselves
Like pieces in a jigsaw puzzle a child forces into place
On a boring, rainy, April morning,
All of which reads, he says, like hieroglyphic scum
On top of this great pond, while underneath,
He does not say, all that lives
Swims a slow and noble, ordinary, translucent life,
And all that dies falls to the bottom and becomes food.

I don't want to sound like the insensitive big shot
With his small ideas, but it's not
The mass killings in the world's fields
With reductive mathematics that matter as much
As that principled woman in the newspaper's second section
Who refused to do her housework
For ninety-seven days to prove a point. What might
She have been thinking the moment her grudges
Turned to a firm resolve, the second her hand
Picked up the dust mop and began its familiar
Sway and dance across the floor, then stopped?
Do people grin when they're alone? If we are to go on swim-
        ming,

We need to know that. It's not the ears
The Colonel collected from his tortured dead
And swept from the coffee table in a gesture
Of contempt to terrorize the visiting reporter,
But how an ear might have felt if only the reporter
Had thought to bend and gently pick one up
And lay her mouth down to ask for the gossip of death.
Break the ice, human nature oozes out, that poetry
Somebody called *the gossip of the inner life.*

John Clare, the mad and minor rural English lyric
Realist, would have loved it, would have lived it,
As he in fact did, in *Poems Descriptive of Rural Life & Scenery,*
Gossip of the badger, the fox, of maids and maidens
And the *Mary* he made up
To remind us of the purity of unrequited love.
What I remember, besides a few quaint, specific
Poems he wrote that never made the evening news,
Is that he once escaped the asylum and walked
Six days eating grass and bugs and weeds
From Epping home to Northampton, and believed
He was the great Lord Byron himself,
"...mad, bad, and dangerous to know."

Imagine, my friend, you are John Clare as Lord Byron
Opening the mansion doors
At 9 a.m., and receiving every guest,
Honored and dishonored alike, John Clare as
The filthy peasant with his hair slicked back
Sitting at table with John Clare as Lord Byron
Who had just come back from hunting grouse and snipe.

And what are grouse and snipe? you should ask.
It's important.
                And what did they say, one madman
To another? "What's new?"
Which is another way of saying,
What's the gossip from the interior?
Who would one day say,
"...now I only know I am, that's all."
And the other would reply, "What! What!"

☉ ARS POETICA

We'd already had a few glasses of wine, and the woman
        wanted to go first so eagerly
She raised her hand like a sixth grade girl, composed herself,
        and began:
"This was years ago. I was taking a plane from San Francisco
        to Boise
And I got stuck on the toilet. I couldn't unglue myself. I
        kept banging on the door
Until the stewardess came and yanked hard on my arm—
        nothing—
And pretty soon there was a small line of passengers, curi-
        ous, horrified, then amused,
Then wanting to be helpful, each of them giving a big yank,
        and *nothing,*
And me getting more and more then less and less embar-
        rassed, then some good soul
Brought me a glass of wine. Lunch arrived on a tray. Then
        they began to pull again,
Gripping each other's hands in an uneven tug of war. They
        were chatting, tipsy,
Getting to know each other, forgetting *my* predicament. I
        could hear them telling
Their own most embarrassing stories, then the clink of
        glasses, laughter,
And so on, until we landed, *Jesus!* and a man in a worker's
        uniform stepped gingerly
Onto the toilet around my bulgy thighs with his *excuse me,*
    ma'am, staring

And trying not to stare, and with a long screwdriver undid
      the entire compartment—
Plastic walls, sink, the toilet itself—and then *pop!* the suction
      released, and I was free.
The sound must have echoed through the plane because I
      heard this terrific applause,
Stewardess, pilot, co-pilot, passengers, clapping, and that
      was it..."

And that was it. It was as though a balloon had been sud-
      denly blown up
And just as suddenly deflated. She didn't seem embarrassed,
      but bashful, rather,
This middle-aged woman, plain and pretty and plainly
      dressed,
Seated with her knees locked together like a newly pubescent
      girl
In a roomful of adults. Then a long pause, a shifting on the
      couches and the chairs,
Then Anne screeched, the way she does when she's confused,
      then some brandy,
Then Eric, the mischievous psychiatrist, called for another
      story, and I started,
But in the middle Gail gave me that look that said the story
      was *more*
Than embarrassing, too much about to be revealed, so I stut-
      tered to a stop.
Inappropriate personal disclosure, Max called it, and I laughed,
Unsure, suddenly, of what actually *was* appropriate—
How open should one be? And where was that line you
      crossed
At your own peril, and of what value was the crossing?

To make us feel more comfortable
In a conforming world? Or harmful, alienating, casting a
person out?

The woman started up again. Her husband, caught in bed
with a man
Prettier than she was...the search for the missing tampon...
the hotel garden in Prague,
One story sliding into another, like someone who, caught
out,
Confesses every sin, every crime, even those she hasn't been
accused of,
And none among us had the courage–if that is what it was–
To give back the dignity she had so eagerly given away,
To say, *No more. That's all we need to know*. "That's all I've got,"
she said.
Now she was blushing, turning a bright red, as though she
had turned herself
Completely inside out, as though she realized that the telling
of her own
Most embarrassing stories was itself *A Most Embarrassing
Story*
Someone would tell later, *on her*, and she wouldn't be there to
sort of *modulate* it.
She started to cry, really sob. Even so, she looked beautiful in
that moment,
Extraordinary, this unprepossessing woman, innocent in her
way,
Like a wet red infant glowing on the couch,
The way we would have been if we had no secrets,
We who were still complex, and secret, and proud.

◉MONKEY MIND

When I was a child I had what is called *an inner life*.
For example, I looked at that girl over there
In the second aisle of seats and wondered what it was like
To have buck teeth pushing out your upper lip
And how it felt to have those little florets the breasts
Swelling her pajama top before she went to sleep.
Walking home, I asked her both questions
And instead of answering she told her mother
Who told the teacher who told my father.
After all these years, I can almost feel his hand
Rising in the room, the moment in the air of his decision,
Then coming down so hard it took my breath away,
And up again in that small arc
To smack his open palm against my butt.
I'm a slow learner
And still sometimes I'm sitting here wondering what my
        father
Is thinking, blind and frail and eighty-five,
Plunged down into his easy chair half the night
Listening to Bach cantatas. I know he knows
At every minute of every hour that he's going to die
Because he told my mother and my mother told me.
I didn't cry or cry out or say I'm sorry.
I lay across his lap and wondered what
He could be thinking to hit a kid like that.

☺ONE-MAN BAND

What was wrong with me that I couldn't sit still
The way the rest of them almost could?
Couldn't contain myself; couldn't hold a thought
About the Emperor Claudius of Rome, or Mozart,
Or the simple abridged anatomy of the birds
Soaring over the schoolyard; couldn't hold onto the numbers,
What they indicated without their indicators,
Numbers that appeared on the chalk board
And disappeared as quickly as the birds themselves;
Couldn't string one thought together with another thought
So the world would make the kind of temporary sense
Children begin to compose a world of.
I whispered constantly, sometimes to myself,
Passed silly notes to my neighbors
Who sat so close across the aisle
You could smell their morning breaths,
All of us lifers, imprisoned in our little desks
Practicing for what we must have thought would be
A lifetime of enforced composure. I ground my teeth,
Picked my nose until it bled, cracked my knuckles,
Played with words in my head so they became as real
As the toy soldiers I arranged and re-arranged on the rug;
Twitched, jiggled my knees, shifted positions in my seat
In a sort of strut, a military march in place;
Stretched my neck until it felt as though I might
Fly out of my body towards my blurred reflection
In the shut windows like the birds did,
Retracting at the last second; and to that camp song,
The shin bone's connected to the ankle bone,
I learned the child's sixth grade irritating art

Of cracking each joint in my body
In a staccato interrupted chord, playing myself
Like a piano or a set of conga drums,
And I thought, *Here's a talent for The Ed Sullivan Show.*
Until the girls tittered, the boys mimed that silent roar
That signals both appreciation for
And condescension to the weird, and the teacher,
A gentle, patient, understanding man, would look up
From the papers on his desk at this one-man band,
This boy dancing in place like a dervish,
And knit his brow and shake his head at me,
And mouth, *Settle down!* Then I would explode
Out of my seat and rush
Down the aisle to the big window in the back
And sharpen my pencil until there was no pencil left,
And, glaring out across the lawn, compose myself
By trying, with all my might, to watch the grass grow
And force the iris from its edging bed.
Until the spasms rhythming my body
Would stop, and the only song was faint bird song,
And its background, the comforting atonal susurrations
Of cotton trousers, cotton dresses,
And my body and the world
Were returned to me for at least a while.
So it was with my father; so it is with my son.

LEARNING HOW TO LOOK:
RILKE & RODIN

The tiny snails of sweat dripping from the underarms
Of Lisette pulling taffy in the window of a shop,

And the *émigré* Russian midget leaning in earnest,
Doggy, whispered conversation with the muzzled mastiff

Hulking at his side, both scratching idly at their fleas,
And there's Etienne the safecracker brazen

In his daytime clothes, casually studying the signs
Of the shops he passes, so you think him

A tourist on the wrong street, this back street
Whose name only the students know, and here come

The bastard children of the prostitute
Walking behind her in parade from smallest to tallest,

Gypsy up to blond-haired proper English gentleman,
And the killjoy from Normandy sweeping the sidewalk

With his whiskered broom, and his one apprentice,
The indolent, sluggish teenage boy who, seeing

The prostitute, sorts the nails and screws
With unaccustomed gusto into the barrel

On his left and the barrel on his right,
And the Israelite butcher with his apron of blood

Bearing, like a bouquet of daisies to a sweetheart,
The musky gore and trimmings to the old widow

With eyes like dried up puddles who hunches
On the curb slicing the corpses of onions into a pot,

And there goes the lopsided cynic with his tomes
Clustered in his arms like sheaves of unhusked corn,

Twitching in homage to St. Vitus,
Where is he going, where are all of us going

But back and forth and forth and back,
And here comes Monsieur Rodin, Francois Auguste Rene,

In case you asked, with a style of stone
In his forehead and his nose, the foolish sculptor

Who should have been a plain mason
Because there are the steps to be patched

Leading down to the Seine, which scolds us all
For our coming and going, and we sometimes wonder

What an *artiste* is doing in this *arrondisement*
Dressed in his ritzy squalor, eyeing the passersby

As though we were undressed and beautiful
Perennial stone flowers, and two steps behind him,

Herr Rilke, his short, pale, undernourished, neurasthenic
Austrian apprentice who thinks he loves us all,

Is trying to keep up, in little hops and skips,
And taking notes on learning how to look.

◉ THE PAINTER

Clouds, and between them, sunlight scattering shadows on
    the road,
Then, when the road curved sharply, flowers, wild flowers,
    yellow poppies
Startling and spotting an upland meadow, surprising me out
    of my thoughts.
We'd been travelling. I had a little job to do. Gail had made a
    reservation
And the motel lady said it was for one night only, they were
    booked,
But the next morning there was a vacancy and the lady said,
    shaking her finger
Like a stern schoolteacher, *Don't forget to move your car*
When you switch rooms! We have only so many parking spaces.
We changed rooms, moving our small belongings, setting up
    house,
And there we were on a day trip to a ghost town on the
    mountain road
And there was the meadow, and I pointed—*Gail, will you look at*
    those flowers!
She had that look that said she was visiting another place
    inside her head,
A better place, a counter-universe where a painter could
    arrange
And rearrange flowers into birds that flew, the mountains
    into buildings
On the streets of Paris where the light had been so beautiful,
    so baffling,
Fixing its shadows to the stones, losing the stones and gain-
    ing more light,

That it drove her even further in. *I'm a tourist of the interior,*
　　　she told me then.
Paris. She had walked relentlessly and daily for months, stop-
　　　ping, gazing,
Dreaming, lost beside the Seine beside the sleeping *clochards,*
Making sketches, rushing back to our apartment to paint, to
　　　arrange
And rearrange *because,* she said, *the real world is just too much*
　　　for me.
I can't deal with it, and she would come out only for a moment
Because I asked and I asked because I didn't want to be
The only sane person left walking on the *Place de la Republique.*
Now she looked out at the yellow poppies and said, *What*
Are they doing there? Then she said, *Uh-oh! We forgot to move*
　　　our car!
And I said, *Gail, we're in the car!* And she started crying.

BUTTERFLIES THAT SAVE US FROM OURSELVES

It came in pills, the mescaline, very fat, imposing, translu-
        scent capsules,
And inside, the blue powder which promised, Jon said,
To revert us to our true characters, then went into the bathroom
With a pile of books, ran the water, and lay in the tub,
Calling out every once in a while, *How's everybody doing?* Gail
Disappeared down the corridor. Linda in the parlor
Stripped off her blouse exposing big round nipples that
        seemed,
As the drug began to take effect, to be growing larger and
        darker—
Wine-stains on a white bed-sheet, I thought. Skin like lu-
        minescent ice,
And underneath, the blue streams, and in them red finger-
        lings
Swimming, I thought, toward the source. The source! But
        what was it?
Our characters, Jon had said. *Who are we?* I asked Linda,
And she said, *Take off your clothes*, which I did, and we started
        playing doctor—
Not sex, but she said *Let's look at our bodies close up*,
And when I got a hard-on, she said, *Let's meditate.*
That's when I heard the noise. A terrible sobbing, then a
        deep
Replenishing breath, more sobbing, and whether it was ema-
        nating
From inside me, or outside, I couldn't be sure, so floated
        down the corridor,

Feeling *beside myself*, and on the journey some of the bad things
I had promulgated onto others
Were riffing through my brain like speeded-up scenes
In a Laurel and Hardy short. My father in his striped pajamas
        yelling.
My mother on the sofa darning socks, moving her mouth
The way she used to, but no words. A woman walking toward
        me
And a woman walking away, different women then the same,
And through it all the same one-note song, *I hate myself.*
Then there she was, Gail, curled up on the bed. *What's the
        matter?* I asked.
She said, *I have no pockets to put my thoughts in!—*
Then I was stroking her hair, trying to make nice like a child
        will
With a traumatized adult, watching the bad thoughts
Spasm across her face. Then Jon was turning the thin pages
Of a book of Japanese water colors. Translucent and pale
And layered. The land moving up and the land moving down,
Whiskered with clouds, and scattering here and there
Specks that could have been people or could have been butter-
        flies
And I thought, or I said: *This is as long ago as long ago gets.*
And sure enough it seemed to take hours, this viewing,
As though we'd all our lives been looking at these pictures.
This was our country and they were our landscape. Jon would
        always be
Subtly altering the landscape because that was his job. Gail
Would always be crying, but more softly now,
And we would linger there forever, somewhere in the sixties,
Out of the weather of time and before we reverted
From our true characters to the rest of our true lives.

◉ THE GREAT WHEEL

What ever became of the people from the 1960's?
What happened to the young man
From a well-off family in the east,
Who had tried college and found it wanting?
Each night waxing and polishing
The hallway floors of the English Department,
Where I was, and still am, teaching,
He looked very busy, all the labor
Concentrated in his narrow shoulders,
Trying to both control and let loose
The heavy polishing machine in its back and forth
Swathing across the linoleum, a hippie, long-haired,
An unlikely night maintenance man, making a mirror
Which would become dirty and blurred
Again in a week, and I deemed him purer,
More innocent than I.
                                        Once, he rapped
At my office door and showed me his poem,
Hand-written, on the several lined sheets
Of a yellow legal pad. It was terrible stuff, more
Manifesto than poetry, full of
The powerful feelings of political expedience
In the guise of political commitment.
I suggested that he put a waterbed in one line,
And the roach of a marijuana cigarette
In another, and that tall, sensual, homely girl
We both knew from the bar
We all used to drink and play pool at, in another,
And to include the dark spaces between her teeth,

For which he thanked me profusely,
Thinking me an expert.
                              Then I suggested
That he not use the word *revolution*
In its commonly-used sense
Of replacing the Government of Old Ideals
With the Government of New Ideals,
But as a word for change, as in *rotation*,
Like a fan belt, or a wheel:
How everything goes around and comes around,
As the working people he admired would say.
And although he looked hurt,
He thanked me for that, too.

I never saw him again, either in the English Department,
Now called the Department of English, or in the bar
We hung out in, still called The Shanty,
At that time filled with the poets and painters,
The street people who arrived from everywhere in America
Just to hang out and *be*, and the few elderly pensioners
From the neighborhood who thought we were crazy
But loved it all, for the coursing energy
Fueled by the music, the drugs and the sex
You could almost smell it was so easy.

Tonight, I sit in my same office,
Hearing the same heavy, humming, *swish swish*
Of the polisher in the hallway outside my door.
Strange, how memory works, how it serves us
And doesn't serve us. I hope the scientists
Will never lay bare the gears and pulleys of its chemistry.
Strange, also, poetry, how, as with memory,
You start with a first thought, a gist,

A ghost of a question, and you wonder
Where it's headed. For example, will that tall homely girl
Grow up to be a woman? Will she get her teeth fixed?
Will she remember us who secretly desired her,
Homeliness and all? How much of the brain's chemistry
Is narrative and how much imagination
Nudging narrative along? What is it
The poem is getting at? The nature of work
Or the nature of change? The transience of ideology
Or the poetry of transience?
Or memory itself, in the way it *constitutes*,
How a shape will rise
Up out of the electron stew
Into a noisy hallway and become
A young man again, with an iffy future,
Doing his labor so that I may do mine.

REVERIE: THE GRAVEYARD SHIFT

When I was waiting for my life to start,
There was a man I traded pants with once,
A black man on the graveyard shift

At Spaulding Sporting Goods where all night
We did what they called "women's work" because
It required a manual dexterity most men

Weren't capable of. We would do it, or we tried to,
Seated at old-fashioned Singer treadle sewing machines
Under a light dispersed by dust and idle thought.

We would turn, in place of a spindle,
The cardboard-covered shaft of a golf club,
A cheap one for the rising working class

So they'd have something to do
Saturday mornings besides an extra shift at the paper mill
Or mowing the lawn again. We would stroke-tap

The treadle with one foot, the way you stroke
A pool cue, the black man told me,
Or the way, an old man confided in me there,

After his heart attack, he re-learned how to make love;
And with a small paintbrush dab some Elmer's Glue
On the shaft, and, still tapping the treadle, we would wind
     down,

In a smooth gesture I would never get the knack of,
A leather, or imitation leather, half-inch wide black strip,
Which was the golfer's grip, neatly pocked

To create some suction for the golfer's sweaty hands.
We would spiral that strip down so the edges lapped,
But didn't overlap. Impossible! Looking back,

This was strange and meaningless concentrated work
For men who would never, now that I think of it,
Play a round of golf. They would never,

Most of them, rise to the middle class. And it amazes me
That I can remember this, not the events
Memory captures in its big net,

But the shop vocabulary, and the light,
And the friendliness of the sleepless
That made of our useless work an ambience

I can call back in a poem from thirty-seven
Forgettable years ago when I went to work
In order to go to college, as I would go to college

In order to work a better job.
The guys nicknamed me, gently, as they nicknamed every-
        one,
Or so I thought, and with a respect tinged

With what I now hear as innocent awe, *The Poet*,
Because when the foreman drifted off
To his smoke break I read Horace

For the cruel clarity of his odes,
And Gerard Manley Hopkins for the stuttering God
He made up out of idle thoughts.

I chose the graveyard shift because
I started with the useful error of thinking
That a poet required, besides pencil and paper,

Dim cones of overhead light
And the company of working men, and because
I had a girlfriend who liked to make love

In the day time, daylight,
Outdoors in good weather,
In her father's car in the bad, and because

I loved the phrase *graveyard shift*,
For the effect it had on my mother,
And because the workers were dreamy and drowsy

That late at night, and whenever the foreman
Took his smoke break, which was every half hour
By the clock in his lungs, they liked to tell stories

And I liked to listen, and because,
I forgot to mention in this syllabus of errors,
I wanted to save up the stories for later,

When I would be a poet. This was a time in my life
In between other times, a time of waiting,
The time I traded my pants for the black man's pants

Because I thought his were better, sleeker looking,
Though when I put them on during lunch break
I looked the same as I had before, and in my pants

The black man looked just as good as he had before
Because he carried his clothes well and because
Some people look good in black, even in black skin,

And because he wasn't waiting for anything.
Looking back requires a harsh light
And a cold intelligence. So excuse me

If I have dispersed the light and given reasons,
Especially about men who spent their nights
Fashioning the shafts of cheap golf clubs, who maybe dreamt

Of playing golf themselves one day, so they could look,
Not across the dumb, humming machinery of their labor,
But far, far across the acres of sloping mown lawn

Bounded by trees now faced with a new and honest light.
One morning I did just that. I slid
One stolen seven iron up my new pants leg,

And punched out, and rode my motorcycle
To the golf course, and, lacking a ball,
Took swing after practice swing, while the others

Were already asleep, living their lives.

☉ REVERIE: *THE SATURDAY EVENING POST*

Age ten, I wanted to write those sentimental stories that
      made me cry,
Historical stories I read in *The Saturday Evening Post*
While sitting in the big blue chair next to the Philco radio.
      Historical
Because written in what I was learning was the past tense,
Meaning something had already occurred; sentimental
Because a person could go on with life, a little bit chastened,
      a little bit wiser,
After the story's end.
                  The Saturday Evening Post made me cry
      once a week,
So I wanted to make everyone in the neighborhood cry
Each time they saw a full moon bulging at the horizon,
Or smelled new-mown hay on a Sunday drive,
As my father used to do, out on the washboard dirt roads
Where people lived far enough apart to feel independent,
My father used to say, yet close enough to know
When an old man died or a baby was born or two young
      people
Walked hand in hand at the end of the story.

Even my father, a skeptical man who didn't believe in God,
Who believed that work was the only salvation—
Like all the fathers, insensitive, thoughtless, now that I look
      back on them—
Who was slowly going blind from what I imagined
Was a speck of rot in his eye, would cry
When I sat in his lap and read him a story,

Or we listened to *One Man's Family*. We cried
Whenever something sad happened and sometimes even at
       the happy moments.

I don't remember a single story from the *Post*. They were
       written
Only to give you that burning pinch behind the eyes
And make you, at the end, feel good about your life
Because that was the only one you had. When you finished,
That week's issue got bundled in with the week's newspapers
And when you got a bunch of stacks
You gave them to the Boy Scouts or the YMCA paper drive.

Everything was different, of course, in 1952.
People rarely cursed, and when they did they made the sign
       of the cross
And were immediately forgiven. And the closest a grown-up
       came
To talking about sex was when my aunt once said, *The only
       thing I hate*
About being pregnant is everyone knows what you did.
And time was different, too. All day Saturday the neighbor's
       son
Would polish with a chamois cloth
The shapely silver gas tank of his Springfield motorcycle
Until it shone, and in it, mirrored, you could see my house
With its tall screened windows, and my mother inside, iron-
       ing or baking
Or polishing the silverware. There were paper routes. It
       snowed
More than it snows now. If a boy got in trouble he joined the
       service
And when he came back he was quiet and strong–

The next day he'd be standing in line
With his lunch bucket waiting for the bus with the other
    men.

And no one spoke about the war, or about the last hours of
    Mr. and Mrs. Healey,
Or what the yelling was about behind closed doors, or why
    the Smith boy,
Who had the squashed features of an Asian monkey
And who used to sit all day rocking on his porch,
Suddenly wasn't there. *I wonder what happened to dumb Jimmy,*
My father asked one day, and that was it. Jimmy was part of
    the story.
He had already happened and then the next thing would
    happen,
While out the window the neighborhood spun its leaves
From one season to the next, the snow got shoveled and the
    lilacs burst,
People went away and usually came back, and those who
    didn't
Were still part of the story, except they were history.

Even now, when the dumb god, *Change*, musters his ragged
    army
Every morning and marches them through the streets of the
    neighborhoods,
I'm still a nostalgic man. History cures nothing.
Irony? Perspective? Nothing. *The past,*
As Delmore Schwartz said, *is inevitable.* It sits in its big blue
    chair
Turning the pages of the *Post*, stopping at the jokes
Any innocent could understand, at the ads for TV's
People were beginning to buy because the times were good,

Every father had a job, everything glossy and in black and
     white.

Now, when even the past itself is going blind, hardening and
     blurring
At the peripheries, I have a soft spot for those naps after
     supper,
Sitting in my father's lap, as he was slowly going blind
And before he lost his job, as I rose and fell
With his unlabored breathing, evenings I wanted to write
     about
For the *Post* because they had already happened
And because we were all sure they would happen again.

◉ WHAT I FOUND

After my father died, and the cadaver was shipped off for
    study
At his request, there was business to be attended to,
A visit to the family lawyer, the will to be read, with the
    usual bequests,
The enormous basement to be cleared, by strangers,
Of how many years of unusable detritus,
And from his bedside drawer, the gold wrist watch, his wed-
    ding band, cuff links,
A few old photographs, to be distributed, without dispute,
And from his closet, suspenders, string bow ties,
And curious hats from different eras, different seasons,
To be stuffed into a bag and taken to Goodwill,
And souvenirs—an ashtray from Copenhagen (*To My Friend
    Abroad, 1928*),
And a yarn doll from their honeymoon in Cuba
When Cuba was a place that people went to—
And the brief obituary, dictated by my father months
    before—
Arid, modest, factual—taped to the refrigerator door,
To be taken down after a week, whereupon it disappeared.
So when the prodigal son came home—
I who loved and despised,
I who was loved and despised—
I found nothing but the normalized life
That succeeds the normalized death,
Neither stories told nor tears being shed,
As I sat on the floor in the vast, emptied basement,
Having decided what to take away:
Their love letters (at my mother's odd request),

So corny and sincere they could break a hard man's heart,
And in the palm of my hand the memento
I discovered in my father's desk,
One of those old-fashioned heavy skeleton keys
That in idle moments as a child I used to shift
From one pants pocket to the other,
Never knowing into what locked box or room it fit,
And in my lap
The black yarn Caribbean doll with its bright button eyes.

◉ MY BLUE WOMAN

Some in couples, some alone in that lonely ecstasy
    Dancing can incite, and women with women,
Knowing each other's steps by heart, and old men in overalls
    Swinging little girls in white communion dresses,
Dancing to that odd and loud, astringent, nasal Cajun music
    Merging hills with mesas, flatlands with bogs
And river valleys, tundra, steppes and jungle with this small,
    Neat green lawn behind a wooden church
In bayou country. Off to the side, the band, Mr. Squeeze Box,
    Mr. Washboard, Mr. Harmonica, Mr. Four Spoons,

And I had this thought that all human life down the millennia—
    Root-diggers, spear-hunters, those who moved the goats
From pasture to pasture, and moat-keepers, scribes
    On their high stools, my ancestor who forgot
He was a fisherman from Dvuretz on the Pripet and fought
    In Napoleon's army, and the saleslady down at Sears—
Could be heard and seen in that Gabarelli button accordion
    Expanded and contracted by an elderly, bone-thin,
Blue-skinned Cajun at a Sunday picnic
    I stopped by the side of the road to watch. I've been

To a Karaite wedding in Bucharest. At an Armenian picnic
    Outside Boston I watched an old man slicing onions
Slice his thumb to the bone then call for a needle and thread.
    At The New African Baptist Church I spent
One wild Sunday morning watching the congregants
    Writhe on the floor and speak in tongues.

On the Har Hamenuchot I asked a bearded man
  His native language. *In the street, Hebrew,*
The language of the Torah. To my wife, Russian. But when I dream,
  I dream in Yiddish. I've wanted to meet everyone

Because I didn't know exactly why, and because I read
  In a genealogy book that every human being on this
    earth
Is at least a fiftieth cousin to everyone else,
  And was amazed. The rape of that Korean woman
In a bamboo hut in the middle of a war, her daughter
  Searching out the rapist her father
Fifty years later in The Home for Retired Japanese Soldiers—
  There he was, a harmless little gentleman in pajamas.
She didn't know what to say so she said *Papa?* Those Jews,
  Stranded for twelve centuries on the China coast,

By now with flat noses and epicanthic folds, entirely Chinese,
  Except for that one young man with a head of kinky,
Mediterranean hair—*A gift*, he said, *from my honored ancestors.*
  And that white man's bones thousands of years old
Pre-dating and annoying an Indian tribe in the Northwest.
  How did he get there? Did he have babies
With a local woman? Are we all really related? Squeezing in
  And squeezing out, that accordion's wheezy gospel
Seemed to mean that the farther you get from home
  The closer you get to yourself. Paper cups

Of foamy beer, crawfish *étouffée*, coffee laced
  With chicory and rum, and soon enough
I was invited to dance by a blue-skinned, gap-toothed,
  Heavy-set young grandmother who wouldn't stop

Grinning at me. I thought she wanted to eat me up.
       She called me *Brother!* Then she called me
Cousin Coon Ass! She yelled *gumbo ya ya*. She sang
         Who stole my monkey? The accordion was invented
By a German. The music was African, Creole, Zydeco,
         American Country Western and blues and rock & roll,

Even some Polish, like a polka. I kept thinking of
         That one man's bones, that hunter or shepherd
From a place they probably called *Here*, a dreamy fellow
         Who must have looked up at a bird winging west
And turned right at the river instead of left, and got lost,
         Got scared, got lonesome, set out on a long walk
To find a woman or end his line. I thought I was
         Related to that man. My blue woman
Was shimmying, going *whoo! whoo!*
         In a language anyone could understand.

◉ NATURE RARELY CONFIDES IN ME

The pomegranates slicken after a rain. I know what color
      they are, exactly,
Because I once had a magenta 300cc Honda motorcycle that
      glistened
In daylight and dimmed at night, like these pomegranates.
The birds love them and peck at them.
Then one drops, a pomegranate,
Somehow both slowly and suddenly,
And if you're lucky—which I am—
You're sitting on a hard slatted bench in the yard one evening
      after supper,
Learning how to sit and see.
Why are you so argumentative? my wife had said.
Why don't you go out in the yard and stare at the pomegranates
Before we get into a fight.
I looked up the spelling, first.
                           I had a girlfriend in 1964 I've
      never forgotten.
Excuse me, but here in the yard I can still see the color of her
      nipples
And her black pubic hair curling up from her pale white skin,
And the splatter of cum on her thighs.
I wonder if it's raining where she is? Then I wonder
If she's bending over a sink, doing the supper dishes
Like my wife is and I wonder if
She still wears that perfume that smelled like lilacs after a
      rain.

The past: that's what I think about while meditating on the
        pomegranates.
That's when the trouble always starts. The past is all we've
        got
When we haven't yet learned how to sit and see.

If you've never seen a pomegranate, the insides are packed
With sections of luscious-looking seeds
Separated by yellowish membranes,
For some reason Nature has yet to confide in me.
If you put one on a plate and peel back the thick rind
And dig out a few gelatinous seeds, they taste sweet and wet,
Though dry, like wine.
I'm learning how to taste, too.
It has something to do with paying attention
To the wet slick walls of your mouth,
The way you can taste certain words in foreign languages.
My wife says, *Eat slower, you'll figure it out.*

                                My mind tries
        to sit still,
But it won't, like this poem that wants to be about pome-
        granates
Because they have their own incomparable, lumpy, asyme-
        trical beauty,
Nothing like a woman's or a motorcycle's.
When I was younger
I used to whiz through the dawn on my way home
From the *Wall Street Journal* printing plant
Where I worked the graveyard shift, proof-reading.

I'd pick up my girlfriend and we had a secret spot to go make
      love,
A blackberry bramble some kids had made tunnels through.
We did it so often it made her sore. We did it so much she
      cried out once,
This is not natural!
               Back then, back east, there were no pome-
      granates
To instruct me in color, so the lady at the Motor Vehicle
      Registration
Followed me out to the curb and said,
It's colored magenta. And, *That's some*
Pretty machine for a boy to own.
All that night I corrected *The Wall Street Journal.*
If I saw the word *magenta*, I'd have recognized it.
If I'd have seen the word *pomegranate*,
I'd have been impelled to look it up.
Back then, words were everything to me.
That's when the trouble always started.
My girlfriend would say, *Why don't we take a walk instead?*
And I would say something like, *If you say the word* walk *seven*
      times
You'll sound like a crow by the side of the road. Tonight I'd say,
Did you know that different languages have different onomatopoeia
For different bird songs?
              So far only one pomegranate has fallen,
And it's dark by now, and if I were a Chinese poet instead
      of an American poet
I'd be satisfied. Maybe I'd want to go into the house and hear
      my wife say,
What did you see? Did you learn anything? And I would say,
Nature rarely confides in me. Or I might say,
To travel well is better than to arrive.

And my wife might say back to me,
On a withered branch a crow is perched
In the autumn evening,
And be satisfied.

                  Before dawn, I used to whiz through the
      dark, slick streets,
My mind full of sex, my mouth full of words like *World Bank*
And *Gross National Product.* One infamous poet, on his death
      bed,
Said something like, *I died of too many words.*
And my wife,
A practical woman I love
Sometimes even more than words, says, *You think too much,*
And, *Be careful of that shirt. The stains are so hard to get out.*

ACKNOWLEDGMENTS

I'd like to thank the Guggenheim Foundation for a grant that allowed me to finish this book. And thanks to some friends who graciously read these poems in manuscript & offered suggestions: Charlie Baxter, Roger Bowen, Michael Collier, Tony Hoagland, Philip Levine, Boyer Rickel, Ellen Bryant Voigt, Gibb Windahl, & Jody Zorgdranger.

And my love to other good friends, who offered inspiration by being friends: Tina Feingold, Mike Mayo, Nancy Pitt, & Bill Van Every.

My thanks to the editors of the following publications in which versions of these poems first appeared:

Agni: "Happy As I Am"

The American Poetry Review: "Learning How to Look: Rilke & Rodin"

The Barrow Street Review: "A War-Time Yard"

The Gettysburg Review: "Onomastics & The Falling Snow"; "In the House of the Voice of Maria Callas"

The Greensboro Review: "Reverie: Foreign Movie in a Foreign Country"

The Harvard Review: "The Beach at Nice"

The Massachusetts Review: "Reverie: The Graveyard Shift"

Ploughshares: "Gossip of the Inner Life"

The Princeton Chronicle: "My Blue Woman"

Sonora Review: "*Kristalnacht*"

The Southern Review: "Song: The Kiss"

The Yale Review: "Taboo"; "Monkey Mind"

The Breadloaf Anthology of Contemporary American Poetry (University Press of New England): "Onomastics & The Falling Snow"; "The Great Wheel"

Poets Respond to Violence in America (University of Iowa Press): "Happy As I Am"